Richard Rodney B

THREE PIECE SUITE

for alto saxophone and piano

Novello

Three Piece Suite for alto saxophone
and piano is a transcription made by the
composer in 1996 of three movements
from his Four Piece Suite for two pianos
of 1974. It was first performed on 21
March 1996 by John Harle (saxophone)
and the composer in the Assembly Hall,
Loughborough, UK.

Contents

Duration ca. 10 minutes

THREE PIECE SUITE

RICHARD RODNEY BENNETT

1. Samba Triste

4

Ped. _____

3'20"

2. Ragtime Waltz

(Homage to Scott Joplin)

3. Finale

20

Published by Novello Publishing Ltd.

12/12 (185441)

3'00"

Nov. 9. '95